3 4028 07920 7230
HARRIS COUNTY PUBLIC LIBRARY

JPIC Beckst
liam

D1489338

$6.95
7363295
01/30/2012

Crumbs
on the
Stairs

Migas
en las escaleras

A Mystery

Escrito e ilustrado por
Karl Beckstrand

para Gregory y Hysen

This book available in English-only, Spanish-only & ebook versions: Premiobooks.com

Spanish vowels have only one sound each:
A = "ah"   E = "eh"   I = "ee"   O = "oh"   U = "oo"
In Spanish, the letter J is pronounced as an English H (and the letter H is silent). Qu sounds like a K, and ll sounds like a Y (or a J, in some countries).

Aunque se escriben diferente, todas las palabras que encuentres en inglés en este libro y que terminen en -ear, -ere, -air(s), -are(s), y -aire tienen el mismo sonido al terminar: -er. En inglés, la H no es muda: se pronuncia como la J de español. Crumbs se pronuncia: kramz.

Crumbs on the Stairs
Published by Premio Publishing & Gozo Books, LLC
Midvale, UT, U.S.A.
Text & illustration copyright©2011 Karl Beckstrand

Printed by Sunrise Press, LLC, Sandy, UT, U.S.A. Batch number 10771

All rights reserved. This book, or parts thereof, may not be reproduced or transmitted in any form, —except by reviewer, who may quote brief passages or sample illustrations in a printed, online, or broadcast review—without prior written permission from the publisher.

Library of Congress Catalog Number 2005939080
ISBN-13: 978-0-9776065-9-7

Images of Linda Ronstadt and the Mamas & the Papas used with permission.

FREE online books: premiobooks.com

Gozo Books

Premio Publishing

Crumbs!

¡Migas!

Cuenta cuántas veces aparece el oso.

Would you care to compare where the bear makes his lair? (Count him!)

...crumbs
on the
stairs!

¡Migas
en
las
escaleras!

Hay migas...

There are crumbs

...en el oso.

...on the bear...

Hay migas en los "círculos" y en los "cuadrados"

There are crumbs on the "circles" and "squares"

GREATEST HITS

(and the tear in the chair).

(y en el descarrón de la silla).

In fact,

iDe hecho,

there are crumbs...

hay migas...

EVERY

...en todas

Y si tú te fueras a fijar
en tu prima rubia, Claire,
¿que hallarías
en su cabello?

And if you
were to stare
at your fair cousin,
Claire, what would you
find in her hair?

who

when

cuándo

quién

where **dónde** ? **what** **qué** how **cómo** why **why** **por** **qué**

Now,
Javier would swear
—if you asked
(with a glare)
just why
there are crumbs...

Ahora, Javier juraría
—si le preguntaras
(dándole una mirada severa)
por qué hay migas ...

...On the bear, and the chair, and the hair of your fair cousin, Claire...

...en el oso, y en la silla, y en el cabello de tu prima rubia, Claire...

Harris County Public Library
Houston, Texas

The End

The bear appears five times (seven, counting the cover).

El oso aparece 5 veces

Fin